Answers From The

Akashic Records

* * *

Volume 9 (of 100)

Down-stepped By Aingeal Rose & Ahonu

Published by Twin Flame Productions LLC

Series Info: 9th in the Series
Answers From The Akashic Records
Library of Congress cataloging in publication data

O'Grady, Aingeal Rose, 1953 –
O'Grady, Kevin (Ahonu), 1958 -
Answers From The Akashic Records Volume 9
Aingeal Rose & Ahonu.
ISBN-10: 1-68323-351-4
ISBN-13: 978-1-68323-351-0

Designed and Edited by: Aingeal Rose & Ahonu
From a session on 7 July, 2013.
Artwork: AHONU.com
Published by Akashic Records Press,
an imprint of Twin Flame Productions LLC
Printed in the United States of America

Dedication

The Akashic Records say
our life is a hologram.
It means that we are all each other,
everything is everything else.
When people say we are a part of God,
that's really incorrect. We are it all.
We are the Mind of God.
We are the All That Is
This book is dedicated to
every one of us!

Table of Contents

Author's Note

Hello! My name is Ahonu, and along with my wife and Twin Flame Aingeal Rose, we welcome you to **Answers From The Akashic Records**. You are probably here just like all of us, searching, seeking, looking for answers to the deeper questions of life.

We have been through the dis-information, the lies, the deceit, the coercion, the power and control that has kept us enslaved for eons. We have been injected with mercury from vaccines, inhaled chemtrail-filled air, drunk the fluoridated water, been bombarded with electro-magnetic radiation, eaten irradiated and genetically modified food, and listened to the nonsense and lies coming from our politicians, priests and teachers. But we always knew there was truth we were not being told. We knew the old ways didn't work, but believed there were no alternatives. So, we continued to obey, and abide by the old rules, and remained enslaved in our own minds, and carried on working 9-5 every day, paying taxes and growing old.

Our world may be in deep trouble and we know we are in a time of major change. We find that some people can move through these changes easily while others struggle with depression, illness and disorientation. We understand that those reading this may have been experiencing the same thing — we have felt it ourselves, and there seemingly was no solution.

For this reason, Aingeal Rose and I decided to invite people to come to weekly group sessions to inquire into the Akashic Records for the purpose of understanding our world, our spirituality, our Earth changes and more. Aingeal Rose had been accessing the Akashic field for over 25 years doing private consultations for people around the world. You are reading the results.

In these volumes of practical spirituality in a changing world, you will find answers to questions about Consciousness, Twin Flames & Soul Mates, Kundalini, Chakras, Gifted Children, Fairies, Healing, Lightbodies, God, Creation, The Future, Inner Earth, Conception, Saints, Longevity, DNA, Marijuana, Free Energy, Famous Deceased, Stress, Prophecies, Prayer, Joy, Christian Sacraments, Alchemy, Dolphins & Whales, Symbolism in your Everyday Life, What the Trees Have to Say, What the Water, the Oceans, the Sky, and the Land has to say.

You will find answers about the Solar System, Crystals, Earth, Evolution, Technology, Luck, Karma, Planes of Existence After Death, Time, Timelines, Ghosts, Spirits, Multidimensional Selves, Sacred Geometry and more topics asked by people around the world.

The answers to these questions became the basis for Aingeal Rose's first book called *A Time of Change* which is available from http://atimeofchange.info. Her 2nd book, called *The Nature of Reality* can be ordered from http://thenatureofreality.info.

For more information about us and our work, go to: https://worldofempowerment.com. There you will find testimonials, podcasts, healing services, home study courses, private consultations, books, audio books, downloads and more.

This is the time for accelerated advancement and we can all '*catch the wave*'. It is our intention that these volumes will help you shift and adjust to the demands of this time period because this time period is offering the potential for great illumination, joy and blessings. We offer you this information from Source via the Akashic Records and hope you will experience peace, understanding, illumination and personal betterment from what is contained herein.

Aingeal Rose & Ahonu
Central Oregon
February 2017

Introduction

About The Akashic Records

The Akashic Records is a '*place*' in spirit, a vast library, where the events of creation and everything in it is recorded. Everyone has access to the Akashic Records where all these answers are held if they are able to tune into them. The Records are a field of knowledge about creation and the movement of our lives. This is why we felt it was the perfect place to look for the answers to humanity's questions.

So, if you have been confused, unsure, uncertain, or just plain curious about life and the Earth — you will find many answers here in these volumes. You will be surprised at the amount of profound content in the form of video, audio and transcripts that we have collected from our many sessions into the

Akashic Records and in our conversations with Source. Indeed, in this series of print, ebook, and audio books alone, we have 100 completed sessions in the Akashic library to date, and each month we add more!

Each session is between 1-1½ hours, making the collection at the moment over 120 hours of deep, loving, life-changing content! Each session contains an average of 40 profound statements from the Akashic Records, bringing the total number of statements to over 4,000!

We believe this is one of the largest collections of Akashic Records content in the world, and we are grateful to be able to offer this information to you during this major time of change on Earth.

Remember, that throughout these sessions, Aingeal Rose was not in a trance and neither was she channeling through any spiritual or psychic entity, spirit, angel or ascended master. She simply down-steps this information and knowledge directly from Source. This book contains the transcript of one of those broadcasts. The transcripts are shown in their original Question & Answer format.

If you'd like to learn how to read the Akashic Records, check out our home-study course here: http://akashicrecords.smartmember.com/course-details

The Session

Aingeal Rose (AR): Welcome to the 9th Akashic Records book in our *Answers From The Akashic Records* series.

… Aingeal Rose says the prayer…

As I was saying the prayer this beautiful soft red light appeared in the room. In the past when this red light appeared, it usually had something to do with a grounding energy or with the Earth herself. It also seems to be a very integral part of the grounding frequency of the planet and also the basis on which plants thrive.

Having said that, I got an image of every one of you as a beautiful being of light.

So, imagine yourself as a standing columnar wave of light: a spirit being, appearing very tall. See yourselves moving across the Earth, floating, near enough to the ground to be part of the Earth's electromagnetic grid but moving freely across the Earth and blessing everyone and everything with your presence. This is what I'm being shown.

It is being shown to remind you that this is who you all were in the beginning and this is who you still are now. It is a presence that you have within you that has the ability to move and bless all living things, just by your very presence, by your intention. The Earth is asking us if we could do that now.

Question One

Ahonu: Aingeal Rose's first book '*A Time of Change*' was amazing, and I'm now reading her next one '*The Nature of Reality*'. It mentions Angels a lot of times. Please tell us what Source wants us to know about Angels and Archangels?

AR: Source is showing me pictures of angels as beings of pure spirit of varying frequencies. Each angel has its own unique vibration, or frequency, and even its own personality. The majority of angels are very, very loving, and very willing to be of service. In fact, I'm seeing them very active and busy in regard to their services.

We all have our own Guardian Angel appointed to us at our birth and that angel is specially chosen because of its particular frequency and its personality to help us fulfill our own unique soul purpose. I mention this in my book.

Our Guardian Angels need to be invited into our lives to a greater degree by our own free will, especially now.

They do many things for us, but they could do a lot more if we were to establish a more conscious relationship with them.

Source was really clear to make the point that each one of our angels is appointed specifically for us at the time of our birth. Each one has its own abilities and gifts that are unique to helping us fulfill our purpose. We're given our particular Guardian Angel because it's the angel that we should be establishing a relationship with.

There are many varieties of Angels. There are Archangels that are angels given specific missions by Source. Those angels have an old and long history. Source made it very clear to us that Archangels are really not designed for our personal use and their interaction with us is rare.

Many of the 'beings' that we have called on and still call on, such as Archangel Michael, have been created by our own thought forms and do come to aid us. Not to say that Archangel Michael doesn't exist, but to say that the Archangel Michael who is known in history, may not be the Michael we have created with our own thought forms and images.

This fact shows us how powerful we are as creators of 'beings' who have qualities of healing and protection which we have collectively created.

I know many people call on Archangels and that is what we're used to, but Source reminds us that it is Source that sends Archangels on particular missions.

Those missions can be planetary, or in other dimensions entirely. Archangels have a very different kind of geometry and frequency to them compared to a 'normal' angel. Archangels also carry particular potencies.

The books that this participant mentioned are available from Amazon.com or from http:// atimeofchange.info and http:// thenatureofreality.info

Question Two

Ahonu: What kind of things can we request from our Guardian Angel?

AR: I got an image of a Guardian Angel laughing. What I'm hearing is that they can help you with anything as long as it's not interfering with something that you need to do for your own mastery. They will help you with anything that is for your good. If you want help with something that is not going to advance you in a positive way, your angel will not support your request.

What it would do instead, is attempt to sway you in a better direction and protect you from going down a path that leads you away from your soul purpose.

For example, when you try to manifest a particular thing and find yourself trying over and over, and it doesn't seem to pan out, or indeed, it seems to be thwarted, then that desire may not be in your best interests right now.

At this point you may want to ask a different question of your Guardian Angel, like,

'Show me what I am meant to be doing' or *'what's the better choice here?'*

Your angel will answer you and help you in anything that will promote the fulfillment of your soul contract. An angel can do such things as create openings or opportunities or chance meetings for you, protect you from harm, give you strong feelings (gut feelings) or new ideas that seem to come out-of-the-blue. It can solve problems and provide miraculous results when it is appropriate to your soul progress.

When your angel seems silent or not listening to your requests, it can be because you are meant to make a choice yourself that will either progress or regress your soul and the decision has to be your own.

Question Three

Ahonu: **If the multi-verse is a hologram, can we say that all creation is a thought in the Mind of God/Source and what we experience as gross matter is an illusion?**

AR: That sounds like *A Course in Miracles* question. We have to realize that we **are** the Mind of God. When we say our life is a hologram, it means that we are all each other, everything is everything else.

When people say we are a part of God, that's really incorrect. We are it all. We are the All That Is, every one of us. We are using consciousness while we are here in a body as a single point of focus, as a single point of attention while we are interested in it. That's an interesting phrase, *'while we are interested in it'*.

Much of this is answered in the last paragraph of my book, *A Time of Change* (http://atimeofchange.info) when Source talks about our decision to go *Home*.

It means to go home to the realization that we are *All That Is*, that we are each other. So, when we say everything is a hologram, it means that contained within us is all memory, all knowledge, and all creation.

What Source wants us to distinguish is that 'Its' Mind is a mind of love and *only* love. It holds nothing else in it but pure love — pure love, acceptance and welcoming. It has no judgment, no banishment, no lack or suffering, no death — just pure creative expansion and expressions of love, beauty, music and celebration.

I need to make this distinction that the Mind of God does not hold anything negative. It doesn't hold suffering, pain, punishment or guilt. This distinction is important because not everything we experience is coming from God's Mind, as God doesn't have dualistic thinking.

When you look at what goes on in the world in general, how we use our minds (small 'm'), how we use thought — we create or rather make, many things in this world that are not considered loving.

Certainly the Mind of God is available to us, but it is our choice to know it or not know it. Because we are made in the image of Creator, it means we can create. We create many things that Source considers illusory, precisely because they are not loving.

When you get to gross matter, the physical body, Source has said to us that the core of everything is Spirit and returns to Spirit.

The physical body is an extension of our individuated Spirit.

In other words, it is our spirit that wants to be individualized until we make the decision to go back into unity. Until then we make the body ourselves. There is no judgment around it, there's nothing bad about it, it is just something we are using until we make the choice to go back to unity consciousness.

The body has turned into the perception of the small self. That's what needs to be corrected in our minds; we have made the mistake of identifying who we are with our physical body.

The physical body is made up of our own thoughts, it is made for a particular reason, and each one of us has our own reasons for doing it. But it is not our Spirit self, it is something that is made *from* our Spirit self, but it is not our Spirit self.

Where we get lost in perception and illusion is when we attach an identity to this physical self that says,

'this is me'.

It is not us, it is something we're using. It is an extension of our spirit for a particular purpose. There is no judgment around it. In fact, what I've learned is to value it. I'm not talking about adoring it; I'm talking about appreciating it. I'm talking about thanking it for its usage, for its service while here. I hope this clears things up for you.

Question Four

Ahonu: What does Source want us to know about crystals?

AR: First of all, all life is conscious at its own level, including crystals. Each crystal has its own personality; they are their own being. Like all things of the Earth, we need to respect them, especially when we disrupt them or take them out of their home. They need to be asked if they want to come out of the Earth or the water.

Crystals have families and some of them don't want to be taken from their families. There are other crystals that want to be used for some human or healing purpose and are happy to be taken for this purpose. As far as their usage, we can't generalize and say that all rose quartz' promote love, for example. The truth is that each crystal has its own personality which is unique to it. Crystals need to be respected as life forms that have a family, that have a function, and that contribute to their environment.

So, before we take it out of its environment we need to ask if it wants to come, and then we need to ask it how it wants to be used.

Years ago we did a class on 'Communicating With Crystals' where people brought their crystals from their homes. It was quite interesting because, for most people, they had never communicated with their crystals. Some of their crystals were happy to be healers, some of them were great with babies, some of them were grounding stones, others asked to be put back in the Earth, some wanted to be put back in the water and some had very negative personalities.

Also, just because a person feels energy from a crystal doesn't mean that its good for them. Many people believe that if they hold a stone in their hand and they feel energy from it, they should use it or buy it, but that's not entirely true. This is another reason why we need to learn to communicate with crystals. Not everyone's body can handle the frequency, or vibrations, of certain stones. Every person is unique.

This is why we are suggesting learning to communicate with crystals especially if you feel the need to use them with clients as a healing tool. You should know if the frequency of a stone is beneficial or compatible with your client or yourself before you begin using it.

You can read more about crystals in a later volume of *Answers From The Akashic Records*. That volume is solely devoted to answering questions about crystals.

Question Five

Ahonu: What is happening in a dream when it seems that you are seeing through someone else's eyes but it appears as if it is yourself? Is this me in another dimension another reality?

AR: Yes, you are seeing through your own eyes in another dimension or in another time/space. This is exactly what's happening. For those who don't know what we are speaking about, it is the belief that we all have many other selves existing right now in other dimensions. Since we are all of creation, we have selves that are experiencing other aspects of creation in a wide variety of other dimensions. That goes for positive as well as negative.

Oftentimes, Ahonu and I hold classes in Quantum Jumping where we jump through quantum doorways into other dimensions to meet our alternate selves for specific purposes. You are experiencing unconsciously what we teach people to do consciously.

I have mentioned our friend Penny Kelly in other sessions. She has done much work in dream journeys, where she has met other aspects of herself in various levels of dreams and in different dimensions. She talks about her experiences in her book called: *Consciousness and Energy, Vol. 1* — http://amzn.to/2jY6z7x

Question Six

Ahonu: Why don't advanced beings from other planets let the masses know that they exist?

AR: You used the words 'advanced beings'. Let's qualify that, because not all beings from other planets are advanced. The advanced ones have been honoring the laws of free will choice in this dimension. It's the same reason we don't see God come down here and live amongst us. Many people want to know,

'Why doesn't God save us?', or *'why doesn't Jesus save us?'*

We have been created with free will choice. So, most advanced beings don't appear because it isn't their job to come in and do so. However, in recent years there has been a dispensation from Source allowing advanced beings to help us in a bigger way than in the past, and some of them have been making themselves known. It is important to say that many of them influence and inspire us as they have permission to do so.

They do this through giving us higher thoughts, through giving us pieces of higher knowledge that we may receive telepathically.

What I'm hearing from Source is that no advanced being will ever just appear, or suddenly come in and tell you what to do, or try to control your life. That is not what advanced beings do. It is the same with your guides. Any being who pops in suddenly and starts telling you what to do, is not an advanced being. Advanced beings are interested in your mastery, and they will give you higher thoughts to support your own creative abilities and power of choice and decision.

Question Seven

Ahonu: Those who are familiar with Aingeal Rose's work with the Akashic Records know that she mentions our 'Rishic' Selves in the opening prayer. What is this Rishi?

AR: The Rishi is the part of you that is a ball of light. In some belief systems it is said that we have levels of ourselves. These levels are as follows:

1. Incarnate Self — that is the you that I'm speaking to right now, the physical self.
2. Angel Self — the part of us that is ethereal and remembers God.
3. Archangel Self — the part of us that has Divine knowledge and has achieved certain powers.
4. Christ Self — the part of us that has become a source of pure love.
5. Rishic Self — The Rishi is equated, in appearance, to a 'SUN'. It is the YOU that becomes a ball of light.

* * *

I'll tell you a story that happened to me a few years ago. There was a woman who interviewed me, asking if I'd go into the Records and ask about certain famous deceased people. At one point she asked me about Gandhi. Gandhi appeared as a beautiful ball of violet light. While some were very spiritual, he was the only one, of all the people she asked me about, who had become a Rishi. And that was how he looked — a magnificent ball of light. (Don't assume by this that the 'orbs' people see are Rishi's — many aren't.)

In a later volume of **Answers From The Akashic Records** we covered this in detail. That volume is solely devoted to answering questions about *"The Famous Deceased"*.

Question Eight

Ahonu: Is it important to surround ourselves with white light?

AR: Yes, it is always important to take care of your aura, and surrounding yourself with white light is one way to do it. It's also a good practice to scan your aura at the end of each day. Just close your eyes and look in on yourself and invite whatever colors need to come in to balance you and fill your aura.

After practicing this simple technique, you will notice shifts occurring on a variety of levels. You should feel much better doing this exercise. Take the time to do this adjusting process for yourself each evening because certainly there are many assaults on our immune systems these days. Source is saying to consider this exercise a matter of your own personal health, just like you would a massage or other self-care. What Source *doesn't* want you to do is put white light around yourself because you are in fear in some way.

In other words, don't have that as your underlying motivation, because if you do that, it defeats the purpose of the white light itself. White light is cleansing and balancing.

Let me explain. You will come to a point in your personal evolution where, instead of surrounding yourself with white light, you will *become* white light. That's really what is desired. You will continue to purify yourself of your own judgments and negativity. You will become harmless in your intentions and in your thoughts. You will never wish harm on anyone, no matter what.

Ultimately, we will all get to a point where we '**become**' love. The love that is Source is what we are really made of, but we have done a good job of splitting that into two in our minds so that we believe we are both good and evil. It's the devil and angel image; you know the one where we have a devil on one shoulder and an angel on the other. It represents the two parts of our thinking. When we finally come to a place where all we're interested in is being love, then we start to become that and only that. That white light itself is its own protection.

Question Nine

Ahonu: What is causing all the disappearances and strange occurrences in the Bermuda triangle? Does it have anything to do with Atlantis?

AR: There is a vortex in the Bermuda Triangle that leads to a portal system to other dimensions. It's a sucking down type of vortex — counterclockwise in its rotation. I have heard that there has been a pyramid or two discovered underwater near that area, and the power of that pyramid could have something to do with the vortex pull.

Many of the things that can't be found have gone into a different dimension. It is in the area where *some* of the Atlantean civilization can be found, but I don't see Atlantis as being the cause of the anomaly there.

Question Ten

Ahonu: Are plants conscious?

AR: Source has told us that all life is conscious. So, yes, plants are conscious, they are very aware, they have feelings, and they can register those feelings. There have been many scientific experiments done in laboratories to show this.

There is one story about a scientist who was studying plants. He hooked the plants in his laboratory up to electrodes to see if they would respond or react to any stimuli. He found that plants were extremely sensitive to their environment.

In fact, one night he was cleaning up after having done many experiments throughout the day. He knew there were bacteria in the sink so he poured a pail of boiling water down the sink to kill them. The moment he poured the boiling water into the sink to destroy the bacteria, all the plants in the laboratory started freaking out.

This was measured by his instruments, some of which went off the charts. It makes the point that all life is conscious. Things that we pay no attention to, unimportant things like destroying '*unhealthy*' bacteria, still registered as a traumatic happening to the plant life '*witnessing*' it.

A meat eater commented on a YouTube video we made not too long ago (https://youtu.be/SLiH74YwiwM) that killing animals was necessary for survival. I responded to point out that plants scream too. Here was my response to that YouTube comment:

Source was saying that there is a difference in motivation when killing something for survival as opposed to killing out of revenge or guilt.

How does Source feel about the killing of animals?

It doesn't approve of it either, but was responding to the current consciousness of the general public which has not evolved past the belief in having to consume other life forms for energy.

We could have the same argument about plant life — it has been shown that plants 'scream' when they are being cut, so consumption has a 'no win' to it when we talk about killing other life forms for food.

Source always speaks at the level It can be heard, and in this case, was suggesting that moving from a motivation and a perceived right to murder for judgments sake, or for the hell of it, is an error and not our right.

Going from the inhumane torture and killing of animals to at least honoring and respecting an animal that is being used for consumption would be a big shift for humanity. Is that the highest form of behavior towards another living creature? No, I agree with you. I am sure NO animal wants to be eaten and no PLANT wants to be eaten either, as ALL life is conscious on some level.

The way the world is now, all creatures consume each other for energy, and this is definitely not a highly evolved consciousness. We have not evolved to the place where we do not consume other life forms. Evolution of consciousness is a process — from what we see in the world today on many fronts — it is a very slow process of waking up to benevolence.

Source, as I have experienced It, is the All That Is, a universal intelligence that has the promotion of love, beauty, harmony and abundance as It's underlying and only principle. Anything that differs from that is a distortion in consciousness.

Further, someone once asked Source about abortion — basically is it right or wrong? Source simply answered,

"ALL life is conscious"

This means that every cell is alive and conscious, no matter what state of development it is at, and therefore it registers what is happening to it. Source did not say it was right or wrong, but it gave us the facts. Obviously if a person could accept the fact that all life is conscious, they may think twice about how they treat life. You will never hear Source judge, but It will give the facts.

Paradise Earth has no killing in it as there is no need to consume anything — in that state of consciousness, most likely we'd be breatharians or perhaps just be a source of light ourselves which is our natural state.

Shifting the existing paradigm of humans from the belief in killing, consuming, guilt, punishment, and all that goes with it is hopefully where we will arrive at some point. Taking a look at history and the plethora of dogmas, programs, cultures and justifications humans have for staying separate, we are looking at a big shift that needs to take place.

Most people don't even love themselves enough to believe they can experience the kind of love I am talking about.

Source does not approve of killing anything and does not distinguish between a 'sentient' being or what is considered to be inanimate. But It will look for any place where It can shift our perception, no matter how slight.

Question Eleven

Ahonu: Did the government conspire to create drugs like cocaine and if so, why?

AR: I'm getting a 'no' on that so we can't blame it all on the government; it is more widespread than that. It's not entirely governmental, there are many private individuals involved. Many individuals have had their hands involved in drugs for many years. There are many independent interests that are creating all kinds of drugs. It involves many countries and many individuals in those countries. There are many artificial drugs that are being made by people themselves, drug dealers etc. who are out for money and there are all sorts of cartels surrounding it.

It isn't that the government has never been involved in making drugs or trafficking. I'm not saying that because they have. But it's not only them. This is the answer I'm hearing.

Question Twelve

Ahonu: The Vitamin B shots and the naturopathic gold supplements that are sold in some health food stores, are they beneficial to our health?

AR: Certainly B Vitamins are very important and very beneficial. Everyone should be tested for B12 levels. Gold supplements are not for everyone. Certain people have allergic reactions to metals. There can be sensitivities to copper and silver also, which is why it is important to be tested.

When you see things for sale like that, whether its gold or B12 or whatever, take the time to go to a Naturopath and get yourself tested. Don't just assume you need them. When you're dealing with metals like gold, silver, copper and zinc, you need to have yourself checked to see what your deficiencies are. Love yourself enough to spend the money to get tested. It's a simple blood test.

Many Naturopaths' take insurance. B12 can help your nervous system and can affect your metabolism. Apparently degenerative, MS-type illnesses and other nervous system disorders are related to deficiencies of vitamin B12. So look it up and have your serum levels taken.

John 14:6: "Jesus said to him, 'I am the way, and the truth, and the life. No one comes to the Father except through me.

Question
Thirteen

Ahonu: What is causing the recent mass deaths of the birds and bees? Are they being poisoned intentionally or is it accidental? What effect is this having on the planet?

AR: We have been asked this before. I had a beekeeper friend call me a month ago because all his hives in North Carolina had died. All his neighbors' hives died also, all at the same time. There are a lot of factors involved in this. One is a fungus; the other is the pesticides and fungicides that are used on crops and stay in the soil. These have affected the bees neurological functioning.

Some other causes are climate related, planetary changes, electromagnetic grid changes and GM foods are also contributing to their demise.

'*Intentionally*' is an interesting word in your question. I don't think anybody particularly intended to kill off bees or birds.

I don't believe the culprits truly understood the far reaching effects on the environment. The good news is there are movements afoot that are banning a lot of these things we just spoke of. That is very, very positive.

The other thing I want to say to you is that, the same gentleman who lost his hives also works with crop circles essences. Interestingly, there was a crop circle that appeared a few years ago in the shape of a bee. He made a vibrational essence out of that crop circle and he took the essence, and we went into the Akashic Records and asked specifically;

'What did this essence need in order to help the bees?'

An essence was created that was designed to restore the bee population. After that he went out and got some new bees for his hive and he fed them this essence. He put it in the bees water to make a sugar water solution, and he started feeding the bees with this mixture.

The bees didn't leave the hive and go out to forage for a while. All of them became very robust and healthy and now they are leaving the hive and functioning well and reproducing. There are now also plenty of nursery bees. So this is working famously for them.

If you are interested in that, you can go to the website: http://NotMadeByHands.com. You can search for the bee essence and if you can't find it in the lists you can call or email Brian Crissey and he'll know what you're talking about.

Question Fourteen

Ahonu: Are there Crop Circle essences for humans too?

AR: Yes, there are many crop circle essences for humans. They're all on the website: http://NotMadeByHands.com When you go there you will see a long list of essences made from crop circles that cover a wide variety of uses. There is everything there to help the human and the Earth on multiple levels.

Disclosure: Having a long time association with the owners of NotMadeByHands, Aingeal Rose was asked to *'read'*, or interpret these essences. You will find her interpretations of each Crop Circle Essence in the Product List. These interpretations were all down-stepped from the Akashic Records.

Question Fifteen

Ahonu: Is the sexual act for the purpose of creating life only, or can it be appropriate for the expansion of love between two people?

AR: What Source is saying about the sexual act is that it is an act of creation. What happens in the sexual union, or the exchange of energies between two people, is a creation. Its a different dimension of creation if you are not creating a child. In other words, your thoughts are creative, your intentions are creative, and your feelings are creative. We could go up the entire chakra system and find creativity at every level.

Every one of the chakras has its own frequency of creation and actually connects to different realities. The sexual act is not strictly for creating a physical person, even though that's the chakra (base and sacral) that you do that from. Creating a human life form should actually be done from all the chakras in unison, but it seldom is.

It wasn't always that way. Back in ancient history babies were created by thought; it was the agreement between both people that formed the new body. I always found that very interesting.

In terms of the sexual energy itself, Source wants us to know that, since sex is an act of creation, the thoughts and images you and your partner are having during a sexual energy exchange has a lot to do with what you are creating. Source wants us to be more conscious of that. So much of our sexual activity is based on fantasy and erotica in some way, and we need to understand that we make entities when we engage in those sorts of thoughts when we are in that heightened state of sexual arousal. We create a likeness of our thoughts and desires and a life form will manifest from that on some level.

I am making this point because Source has told us that most of the negative entities that are floating around are entities that we have created by our own thoughts. However, if you are having sex, and you are completely in a loving space with your partner and you are sharing love, and your thoughts are focused on loving, then of course you are going to create a thought form that is like that. And in those cases it can be absolutely wonderful.

The bigger message that Source is giving me here is that It is requesting that we ask ourselves what our focus and intention is for our sexual activity. Too many people use it because they have no other way to have pleasure.

What Source is saying to us is, you need to know that exploring your own inner self, your own chakras, raising your own Kundalini carefully, actually brings you into higher and higher expressions of pleasure as you move up your own anatomy. There is nothing wrong with the sexual act from the sexual chakra, just to say that there are higher and higher levels of pleasure and loving expression and not to get hung up in one chakra. For those who use sex selfishly or inappropriately, Source is recommending looking into your motivations and clearing your unloving thoughts. One of the ways this can be done is by journalling — see http://tw.smartmember.com/

Question Sixteen

Ahonu: Is divorce acceptable under any circumstances? Can one recover a marriage even under harsh conditions that seem almost impossible to overcome?

AR: Source first wants to define what a real marriage is. A real marriage is a commitment by both people to honor the highest degree of love in one another at all times. It is a communication and an intentional communion. A marriage is a joining in these ways. If this isn't happening, if only one person is doing the communicating and making the decision to join with the other, to be loving, to be honest, to uphold the highest standards for the other, that is not a marriage. It's not considered a relationship if only one partner is willing to join. That might help with the divorce question. When people get divorced it's because one or both are making the decision not to join and not to hold to high standards of love in themselves or each other.

In those cases, if there isn't the willingness, there isn't a relationship.

So, when you talk about divorce, divorce is the result of an unwillingness or an inability to love. Source does not consider it a sin or anything wrong, because it doesn't consider it a relationship when there is a refusal to join. It's easy to see then, that if you have couples who are in a loving, committed relationship, who practice loving, who work on themselves, then you have a marriage. Marriage is the joining of communication, the joining in love.

Having said all of the above, of course anything can be healed. We would never say that healing a marriage is impossible. Anything is possible.

Sometimes when a person is doing a lot of work on themselves, it can also shift their partner. But sometimes it doesn't shift the other. There does come a point where the other or both need to come on-line with one another. Each has to be willing to be responsible for their own mastery and self-growth.

Love is a masterful thing, love is a creative force, and it is a conscious activity. Love is not just a nice attraction or a nice feeling. Love is a conscious, creative decision. If one or both refuses to do that, there comes a point when the opportunity of their relationship needs to be reconsidered.

Question

Seventeen

Ahonu: When you speak of everything coming from within, can you tell us what purpose curses and spells serve and are they karmically related?

AR: Curses and spells don't serve any positive purpose. They are under the heading of something that is considered negative and manipulative, and interferes with another's free will. We could say that lessons can be learned from any experience, but it wouldn't be a lesson coming from love.

When I say everything comes from within, what I mean is that there must be a resonance within a person somewhere with the frequency of a spell or curse if they are experiencing it.

If they are in effect of one now, they could look within to feel that energy, and in doing so, they might find a common resonance with the curse or spell energy and some part of themselves.

Perhaps they would find that they did live in a lifetime where they were doing some of the cursing and hexing as well.

Certainly there were many years where the modus operandi of some of the old pagan and Celtic clans was to put spells and curses on one another, on families and on their enemies. Some of those curses can be inherited through generational lines, and perhaps if a person became aware of them then they are the one that can de-energize them.

Curses and spells have unique energy signatures and they have different vibrations. Source is putting them in the category of vampire energy. If you've ever felt vampire energy you will know it.

Vampire energy is a strange type of hypnotic and alluring energy because it uses the magnetism of the blood to allure. In other words, vampire energy steals the magnetic life force in the blood for its power.

Curses, spells and voodoo also use substances from the person or the elements of the earth for their magnetic power. In the big picture, Love is the ultimate creative force of the universe and it can't be destroyed, ever. So when we feel we are under a spell, or we feel cursed, it is asking us to examine the part of us that still 'owns' hatred, anger or revenge.

When we say everything comes from within, it does in the sense that if we can be affected by something then we've got some sort of similarity inside ourselves that resonates with it.

It isn't that we'd necessarily desire to put spells and curses on someone else, but it can be an issue of power — how we use our own power, or if we feel dominated by others, how much of our own power we give away.

We are being asked to look at our own frequency of anger, hatred or judgment that we may still be holding against people, ourselves or a situation. As long as these are resonating inside us, we can be in effect of that particular energy. Remember, blessings and forgiveness start to unravel and disconnect these things.

Question

Eighteen

Ahonu: Why is it important or significant to incarnate in this dimension?

AR: Source is saying that the main reason is because Source desires Paradise's everywhere. That's the big answer. We first came to Earth as Spirit beings long, long ago before Earth became this dense. The reason we keep coming back now is because the Earth fell to a denser frequency from a cosmic wave that hit it very long ago.

That's the short story, but once that happened, we also digressed in frequency, not really because of any choice but because of the consequence of this event.

For the complete story of *'The Fall'*, see *A Time of Change* (http://atimeofchange.info).

Many of us have been coming here through the various cycles to try to resurrect this planet back to its original frequency. It was a very powerful Paradise at one time.

In fact, there is a piece of it that still lives as *'Paradise Earth'*. We did originally start coming here to Earth on savior missions to try to raise the frequency. You have to think very long-term about the full history of this planet, in terms of its origins, its life forms and its species.

Resurrecting something back to a Paradise frequency once it has digressed involves a long process of evolving the current species and consciousness of a planet. This means *every* life form on the planet, not just human. Many of us have had lifetimes on other systems where we were masterful at science, healing, or genetics and are here now as part of this evolvement process for the species of Earth at this time.

Some of us are here also, to master our own consciousness. When we started coming here, many of us fell into the lower density ourselves. When you fall into a lower density, many times you lose your memory. We lost our memory of where we came from and what we were originally doing, and we got caught up in the status quo of the density of the planet. We started creating karma, we started thinking we were people; flesh people instead of spirit people.

So, there are a lot of reasons why we are here now. Some who are here now haven't forgotten, they know they are here to raise the planet back up; some are here for many other reasons. Some have lived many lives on Earth and this is the time to clear their karma and shift the frequency as much as possible.

The point is that every planet, every planetary system is loved by Source — Source has told us that It delights in all creation. Source delights in new life forms, and when you have new planets coming into being, there are a group of spirit beings that go there to see what kind of atmosphere it has or how they can develop it. Source's intention is that everything be a Paradise.

Question

Nineteen

Ahonu: Are new souls ever created and are they being born on the Earth?

AR: Let's correct that and say new Spirits. What I'm hearing is, there are always new spirits being born, absolutely. It is a constant process actually. The Universe keeps getting bigger and bigger and vaster and vaster. It seems to me that creation right now is on an expanding spiral, so I'm saying yes to that.

Question

Twenty

Ahonu: Was there life on any other planets or moons in this solar system?

AR: Yes, there has been life on our Moon, there's been life on Mars, there's been life on Venus and on Saturn, and I'm sure many other planets and systems aswell. We need to keep in mind that the particular types of life forms on other systems may not look like us. They may not be as dense or indeed, could be denser.

Some of those planets do not have living beings on them (in terms of civilizations) anymore — there's a long, long history here. There are visitors that still come to those places for specific reasons. So, yes, there has been (and still is) life on other planets besides Earth.

Question

Twenty One

Ahonu: Do planets have souls?

AR: They definitely have a consciousness but not a soul in the same way humans do. Source is explaining this in the context of karma. Souls are connected to karmic influences. Let me explain that. When I look at the planets I see that they have a consciousness, that they are living beings, a living presence, however they don't create karma. I find that interesting. The reason is because planets don't make decisions that harm anything else. I don't see war between planets themselves, I don't feel the planets have any intention for any kind of destruction and therefore they don't create karma.

The soul is connected to karma in the sense that it has to do with beings that make conscious choices and decisions one way or the other. The soul gets built. People think their true essence is a soul. It isn't. Their true essence is a spirit. We are all spirits.

The soul is something that gets built by our decisions, by our victories, by overcoming challenges. The soul is accumulative in terms of its greatness or its digression. The planets do not have a soul for these reasons.

Question

Twenty Two

Ahonu: Can Psychic Surgery be done via distant healing?

AR: Yes, Psychic Surgery can be done remotely with permission from the client. Here is a brief explanation of Psychic Surgery, or Psychic Laser Therapy.

Psychic Laser Therapy is a form of psychic surgery that removes interferences from the etheric layers of a client, allowing their true life force energy to flow uninhibited once again.

Did you know that people hold their past lives and karmic patterns in the etheric layers surrounding their bodies?

These patterns reveal themselves as past-life scenes, wounds, belief systems, electrical disturbances, entities, implants, illnesses, missing or damaged chakras and more. These things interfere with the present moment and make manifesting desires difficult. They also cause lack of clarity and confusion.

The result for a client is the feeling of being cleaned and lightened, having quicker manifestations, achieving emotional and mental balance, achieving clarity and renewed purpose.

As well as providing this as a service, Aingeal Rose and Ahonu teach this advanced healing method so you can facilitate greater and more rapid healing for your clients, yourself and your loved ones. This is an important therapy for an important time.

Summary of Akashic Session

1. Archangels are given specific missions by Source.
2. Archangels are planetary, cosmic or universal in nature and are not usually for our personal use.
3. A Psychic Surgeon can work remotely on another person with permission from the client.
4. A marriage is meant to be an expression of the highest degree of love between two people.
5. A divorce happens when one or the other partner chooses not to communicate love at the highest degree possible.
6. A divorce happens when there is an unwillingness to make love the focus of the relationship.
7. Love is a conscious, creative and ongoing decision.
8. The AIDS virus was made by governments in a lab for biological warfare and for population control.
9. The AIDS virus was tested in populations that were considered expendable.
10. There is a deep sadness around death because we don't appreciate the life principle.
11. We are more than a part of God, we are the Mind of God, and the Mind of God is pure love.
12. We are all each other; we are all everything.
13. Do appreciate, but not adore the body.
14. There has been life on many of our planets and moons.
15. Not all beings from other planets are advanced.
16. Advanced beings are only interested in your mastery.
17. We don't see God intervene because we are free will beings.
18. We receive telepathic or higher knowledge to help us make better choices.
19. We have several selves: Incarnate, Angel, Archangel, Christ and Rishi.
20. It is important to nourish your aura and maintain yourself with white light.
21. Consider your aura part of your overall health.
22. Use white light to nourish, not to defend.

23. There is a vortex in the Bermuda triangle that leads to a portal system.
24. Planets and plants are conscious but they do not have an individual soul.
25. Planets and plants are sensitive but don't decide, therefore they do not create karma.
26. There are always new spirits being created.
27. Our true essence is spirit, not soul.
28. The soul is connected to karma through our choices.
29. The soul is accumulative in terms of its digressions or its expansion.
30. Anything and everything for your good can be requested from your Guardian Angel.
31. The Earth was once a Paradise, and an aspect of it still is.
32. Source intends Paradises everywhere.
33. The Fall was a consequence of an event, not a choice.
34. Resurrecting back to Paradise is a long process in which many of us are involved.
35. Many of us are here to master our consciousness.
36. Every planetary system is loved by Source because Source delights in all creation.
37. Because crystals are each their own conscious being and have their own families, we should ask first if they want to be used or taken from the Earth.
38. Many crystals desire to help us; others do not want to be disturbed.
39. Not everyone's body can handle crystal frequencies.
40. Some curses and spells can be inherited through generations.
41. Curses and spells affect those that still own hatred, anger and judgment.
42. The sexual act is not just for creating bodies.
43. The sexual act is an exchange of creative energies.
44. We make energetic life forms in our exchange of sexual energies for good or ill.
45. Many entities are our own creations, arising from inappropriate thoughts during the sexual act.

46. Too many people use sex in the absence of knowing higher pleasures.
47. Every chakra has its own frequency of creation.
48. B-Vitamins are very important to life and people should test for their deficiency.
49. You should always test first for metal deficiencies before taking gold, silver, or copper supplements.

To get one of the thousands of profound statements from the Akashic Records in your mailbox every second day, simply register on the World of Empowerment website here: https://worldofempowerment.com.

Disclaimer

Aingeal Rose or Ahonu does not guarantee that solutions suggested in these materials will be effective in your particular situation. If you are not familiar with any of the steps listed in any solution, Aingeal Rose & Ahonu advise that you do not proceed without first consulting additional resources.

To the maximum extent permitted by applicable law, in no event shall Aingeal Rose, Ahonu or their suppliers (or their respective agents, directors, employees or representatives) be liable for any damages whatsoever (including, without limitation, consequential, incidental, direct, indirect, special, economic, punitive or similar damages, or damages for loss of business profits, loss of goodwill, business interruption, computer failure or malfunction, loss of business information or any and all other commercial or pecuniary damages or losses) arising out of or in connection with the use of or inability to use the materials, including without limitation the use or performance of software or documents, the provision of or failure to provide services, or information available from this document or their websites, however caused and on any legal theory of liability (whether in tort, contract or otherwise), even if Aingeal Rose or Ahonu has been advised of the possibility of such damages, or for any claim by any other party. Because some jurisdictions prohibit the exclusion or limitation of liability for consequential or incidental damages, the above limitation may not apply to you. Always consult a licensed health practitioner for all health issues. Full Terms & Conditions and Disclaimer at https://worldofempowerment.com/wp/terms.

Address all inquiries to:
Twin Flame Productions LLC,
358 SE Sena Ct., Bend, OR 97702
http://twinflameproductions.us

Acknowledgements

So many of you have opened your hearts and minds to Truth, willing to be participants and creators of a new world — a world based on love, cooperation, harmony and peace. And we've had the good fortune to meet, counsel and interview many of you, all dedicated to the empowerment and awakening of mankind. We witnessed your most intimate thoughts and feelings, your fears and strengths, your human-ness!

So, it is for you we have written this series of books, *Answers From The Akashic Records*. You're willingness and thirst for truth has fueled a growth of awareness, allowing for an acceleration in the down-stepping of wisdom and knowledge. Without you, these pages would not have been published, and we would not have had the pleasure of sharing our experiences of Source!

Blessings!

Aingeal Rose & Ahonu

Aingeal Rose & Ahonu
Transformational Catalysts and Spiritual
Visionaries

Aingeal Rose (USA) & Ahonu (Ireland) are transformational catalysts and spiritual visionaries. They are authors, artists, speakers, researchers, ministers, radio hosts and spiritual teachers who, individually and as a Twin-Flame husband-and-wife team, have helped countless people all over the world move from mediocrity to joy, clarity and awareness through their simple but highly effective series of books, programs, workshops and online sessions.

Transformational catalysts and spiritual visionaries, Ahonu & Aingeal Rose, have witnessed their clients breaking free of emotional bondage and observed the light of awareness radiating through their eyes over and over again. This twin flame couple draws on 60 years of combined experience and expertise in self-mastery and ascension mechanics to make a profound difference in people's lives. They are trusted by clients around the world for their authentic down-to-Earth approach, and are known for empowering their clients and helping to raise the consciousness of the world.

International workshops including Mastering Your Destiny, Psychic Laser Therapy, and Akashic Records Training are just a few of the courses they offer. Ahonu & Aingeal Rose are also popular media guests and co-hosts of a weekly broadcast on World of Empowerment Radio. In addition to being gifted spiritual teachers, authors, speakers, and publishers, Ahonu & Aingeal Rose are ordained ministers in the non-denominational Alliance of Divine Love Ministry, bringing that devotion into everything they do.

Ahonu & Aingeal Rose are often referred to as "freedom facilitators," effectively combining spiritual guidance and intuition with eye-opening readings of the Akashic Records. These sessions bring clients into alignment with their soul's purpose and free them from old beliefs that have held them hostage throughout their lifetimes. The Akashic Records are a database direct from Source that answers life-changing questions from each individual's own record of their many lifetimes and sojourns in Spirit.

Along with being the authors of this 100-book series of Answers From The Akashic Records, Aingeal Rose is the author of two other books, "A Time of Change" and "The Nature of Reality." These books share the wisdom from the Akashic Records on a variety of topics that allows readers to discover life-changing insights. Ahonu is the author of "The Reincarnation of Columbus," which is an honest and gripping autobiography telling his true-life story of how a man copes with grief and loss and transforms it into personal empowerment and joy.

Having the unique distinction of being twin flames, Ahonu & Aingeal Rose, share a unique bond that enhances their ability to help others. For example, they offer a memorable and joyful wedding ceremony for couples desiring a celebration that strengthens the Divine masculine and feminine bonds between them. Together they founded Holistic Ireland, the World of Empowerment Organization, the Spirit of Love Project and the 8-Steps-to-Freedom program.

They work throughout the United States and Ireland, are Master Tarot Teachers, an authority on the Akashic Records and hold certifications in Psychic Laser Therapy, Kathara Healing, Soul Retrieval, Reiki and Cellular Re-Patterning. They have held workshops in Manifesting, Self-Healing, Working with Homeopathic Color Remedies, Beginner through Advanced Tarot, Visionary Art and more.

On the https://worldofempowerment.com website you will find testimonials, podcasts, healing services, home study courses, private consultations, books, audio books, mp3 downloads and more. Audio programs are easily downloadable on your iPad, iPod, or iPhone.

For further information or to arrange an interview, book signing, speaking engagement, book a workshop, Spirit of Love painting or Akashic Records consultation, contact them on https://worldofempowerment.com or by Phone USA: +1-224-588-8026 or Skype: ah-hon-u

ahonu@ahonu.com

aingealrose@aingealrose.com

Connect With
Aingeal Rose & Ahonu

BLOG: worldofempowerment.com/wp/
YOUTUBE: youtube.com/user/
ahonuandaingealrose
TWITTER: twitter.com/ahonu
PINTREST: pinterest.com/aingealrose/
FACEBOOK: facebook.com/
newworldofempowerment
LINKEDIN: linkedin.com/in/
kevinogrady

Spirit of Love Project: ahonu.com/
spiritoflove
Spirit Gallery: ahonu.com/gallery/
index.php/spiritoflove
Aingeal Rose's website:
aingealrose.com
Ahonu's Website: ahonu.com
Holistic Ireland: holistic.ie
Sacred Sites Tour of Ireland:
mysticalireland.holistic.ie
Sacred Earth Waters:

SacredEarthWaters.com
World of Empowerment:
WorldofEmpowerment.com

**Ahonu.com, AingealRose.com,
WorldofEmpowerment.com**

More to Explore

Thanks for reading! If you enjoyed this book or found it useful, we'd be grateful if you'd post a short review on Amazon. Your support really makes a difference! Here are more of our works for you to explore:

AKASHIC RECORDS PODCAST
Every Saturday at 10am PST, AHONU & Aingeal Rose discuss each question and answer from this book, and in turn work their way through the entire 100-book series. Listen to the archives at http://answersfromtheakashicrecords.com or subscribe on iTunes here: http://apple.co/2iVxWwq

AINGEAL ROSE & AHONU PODCAST
Every month Twin Flames AHONU & Aingeal Rose interview exciting guests on The Honest-to-God Series on World of Empowerment Radio on the 1st Saturday of each month at 10am PST. Listen to the archives at http://honesttogodseries.com or subscribe on iTunes here: http://apple.co/2j9kaFT

AKASHIC RECORDS — Online Group Sessions
Held on the 1st Sunday of every month online, these group Akashic Record sessions allow you to bring your big questions to Source. ONLY for spiritual/universal/global inquiries of the Universe, not for personal questions. More info here https://worldofempowerment.com/wp/events

AKASHIC RECORDS TRAINING
Accelerate your spiritual knowledge by learning to read the Akashic Records. Come away with skills

enabling you to be an Akashic Records reader. Use the insight and knowledge for your own, your family or become a full practitioner. This is a small intimate training held in the USA and in Ireland — also available online at http://akashicrecords.smartmember.com.

SPIRIT ART
Explore your own Inner Self through art! YOU NEED NO ART EXPERIENCE for this class! AHONU will guide you through various fun-filled exercises that stimulate your intuitive self and inner child to come out and paint! This class is fun, spiritually revealing, and highly transformative. USA and Ireland — not available online. All Materials Provided.

TWIN FLAME / SOUL MATE LECTURE
How do you know if you have met your Twin Flame or a Soul Mate? What are the signs? What is their purpose? Are you in a Twin Flame relationship? What are the challenges and rewards? Includes a copy of our Twin Flames & Soul Mates eBook. This lecture answers these questions and more. USA, Ireland and eBook.

TRANSFORMATIONAL WRITING
This online class will free you from many unwanted belief systems and return your own power to you. By exploring your own consciousness, you will bring many beliefs to light and put yourself in the driver's seat of choice once again. This is a powerful class using a simple tool that is yours forever. Enroll here: http://tw.smartmember.com

PSYCHIC LASER THERAPY for PRACTITIONERS
Within the human auric field are layers of interwoven energies containing a history of our past lives, belief patterns, joys and sorrows and more. The condition of our chakra system and

magnetic web is also held here. These appear as living images and events in our fields, affecting who we are today. This class is a form of etheric surgery designed to remove imprints, blockages, and trauma held within these layers thus freeing your client from lifetimes of accumulative karma. The results are: increased energy, clarity, accelerated manifestation of desires, feeling light and clean and a greater sense of Self. This is a certification course and extends over 2 days — Day 1 is Text and procedure; Day 2 is practical application. This is a small intimate training held in the USA and Ireland — not available online.

THE 8 STEPS TO FREEDOM

This program was originally 8 weeks, starting on the 8 day of the 8 month at 8pm for 88 minutes — it is now online for your convenience and to take at your leisure! Meet with AHONU & Aingeal Rose online as they deliver life-transforming outcomes, make sense of your life, understand your relationships, accelerate your possibilities and help you grow in peace and wisdom. This series was developed by AHONU & Aingeal Rose to fulfill specific desires people need, help deliver specific results people want and to solve specific challenges people have. Visit: http://8-steps-to-freedom.com

Details of all workshops/courses from https://worldofempowerment.com/wp/events

AHONU & AINGEAL ROSE

Other Books by
Aingeal Rose & Ahonu

This is Aingeal Rose & Ahonu's entire book library at the time of publication, and they are publishing more books all the time. Find out every time they publishes a book, by signing up for their alerts below. <u>On Amazon</u> (<u>search for AHONU or AINGEAL ROSE</u>)

Answers From The Akashic Records (in 100 Volumes)
A Time of Change by Aingeal Rose
The Nature of Reality by Aingeal Rose
The Reincarnation of Columbus by Ahonu
Ayurveda, Ayur Veda, Ajurveda
Essential Info About Aromatherapy Essential Oils
Healing With Reiki
Indigo, Crystal & Rainbow Children
Quickest Way to Knowing Acupuncture & Acupressure
Spirit Art, Soul Portraits & Ancestral Healing
Twin Flames & Soul Mates

AHONU has also provided graphic design and editorial support to these authors for the following Amazon books:

Animal Guides, Protectors, Totems, & Power Animals by Chantal Cash
What is Dowsing? By Chantal Cash
Dowsing; An Art of Intention by Chantal Cash

Ensure you get Aingeal Rose & Ahonu's next book. Sign up for book alerts here!

https://WorldOfEmpowerment.com

30516959R00048

Printed in Great Britain
by Amazon